Delightful Daydreaming Nightmares

Arjun Thimmaya

BookLeaf Publishing

India | USA | UK

This book is a tribute to all the daydreamers of the world,

I pray you never stop!

Acknowledgement

I cannot thank anyone at this point,
there is still a long way to go,
My family and friends will make sure that I
find my way.

Preface

Congratulations! If you're alive and reading this... which you are, you already have some luck on your side. For the soul peasants (joyless, tedious, finger-pointers), the belief in the importance of luck overwhelms them only when they sense it is lacking. I don't think you're a soul peasant. Unless you also consider getting lucky requires years of struggling and suffering. No, no, that's hard work.

Life is chaos. The number of permutations and combinations that have worked their way in favouring me or you to be where we are in the world's present scenario is well beyond my limited mathematical capability. Those gigantic odds steer my belief towards pure luck over a divine intervention or an overpowered, all-knowing puppeteer.

Do insecure virgins ever get to inhale their lover's scent? Is a sleepless single child ever reassured by a sibling's gentle snores? Who reads an orphan their bedtime stories or coaxes them out of a sulky mood? Does the presence of a genuine friend sometimes mean more than anything else in the world? These aren't life's little luxuries. Some people just got a taste of luck. There are so many more unfortunate ones, who would exchange all their worldly possessions, for a shot at the real thing.

Pay heed though, daydreaming about the 'lucky' past is a dangerous pastime. Over time, it has a way of corrupting thoughts. Some memories must be held onto like a treasured gem, but polishing it too much will only diminish its value. We must strive to make even more gems, to create and have them flourish with others. Else, one day, there won't be anything for us to be fondly remembered by once our 'luck' runs out completely. Heck, if something makes you fleetingly smile once in a while... you're lucky.

Being afraid of heights, suffering from a deadly case of arachnophobia are all by-products of generations of evolution/ trial and error/ hit and miss/ pure fucking luck. Respect it and listen to intuition. Someone got lucky before us, literally and figuratively, hence we are. Hence we are here today. However, another type of fear is the real enemy. The fear to smile and risk vulnerability. The fear of feeling good now because it might hurt a little later. This fear weakens us, makes every day tedious. It transforms the adventure of life into a waiting room. We must treat a mental routine like a slow-moving stealthy foe; you won't even feel it bleeding you dry, up until it's too late.

'Nonsense', you ponder. What if it actually is too late? What if luck just isn't finding its way to you? What if you can't do anything? What if there is no escape? Now, I must lean on the tough-loving thoughts of the legend himself, *Hunter S. Thompson*, who pointed to the only two choices one faces in life:

(a) Realise that change is imperative in improving one's existence and, more importantly, incorporating said change as quickly as possible.

OR

(b) Gracefully accept that the present state of one's affairs has been brought about due to our own inaction and learn to accept things for the way they are.

Everyone else seems to be doing it, right?
But we don't need to live life like a victim. Dear reader, when luck does come knocking, you might not hear it. Or you might be tending to a different door. Be careful; the knocks will be faint. You must let luck in. Grab it and make the change you know you owe yourself. Don't die a soul peasant.

-Arjun

P.S. *'Luck' = Good Luck, We'll ponder 'Bad Luck' on a distant day*

Spurned

A tiny kitten frolics through the garden,
Dead birds form a feast from heaven,
The kitten is all grown up,
Flicking its tail and licking a scallop,

The biggest fish in the smallest lake,
Might just be the reason for all his heartache,
The lioness bathes in sunshine,
Her caress could end a bloodline,

For every gift the mad prince gives the maiden,
The beautiful girl accepts with a thunderclap,
Only her flesh he cannot partake,
For she will disappear beholding the moonshine.

The Sea Ghost

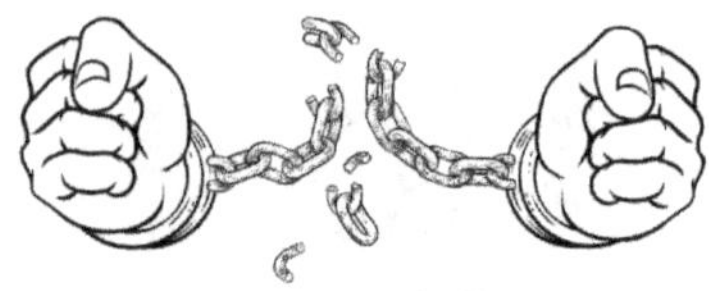

They imprisoned me for a crime of passion,
All I did was just kill him a fraction,
The fighting, the violence, the bullying,
Seeking some peace I hit the Warden whilst curtsying,

Placed in solitary,
Have I become such a monstrosity?
A tiny rectangular box on the top of a hill,
No place to stand or sit still,

Flesh and bone begin to melt,
Time bends itself while I knelt,
I flow through the drains,
Now fluid through the sewers,

Into the sea,
Floating to be free,
Now I am a Sea Ghost,
Hear me sing when you sail beyond the King's post,
Jump in with me and share a toast!

The Legend of Paruti Prasad

Yo-ho-ho!
Gather around!

Yo-ho-ho!
Settle down you dirty bloodhound!

Yo-ho-ho!
Listen to the legend of, Paruti Prasad!
There once was a man,
There were many of his clan,
But none like, Paruti Prasad!

Yo-ho-ho!
He drank rum like it was water,
He was so good he drank it without a spotter!
No one could drink like, Paruti Prasad!

Yo-ho-ho!
One night he drank quite a bunch,
Decided a window needed a punch,
No one could punch a window like, Paruti Prasad!

Yo-ho-ho!
His hand was bleeding,
But so it bled like rum,
The innkeeper was dismayed,
He threatened it would be conveyed,
No more drinking,
No more window-punching,
All it left was Paruti Prasad grunting,
No one could stop, Paruti Prasad!

Yo-ho-ho!
The innkeeper was rude,
The minute he laid his claws he was screwed,
When the one-punch-wonder was removed,
The innkeeper was now in the midst of a feud,
No one could muttonchop, Paruti Prasad!

Yo-ho-ho!
Just as our hero's ass landed on the pavement,
A storm brews as if to form a statement,
For one window broken,
The mighty wind laid all to be rebroken,
Now each window in the inn was but a shard,
The innkeeper was sorry for who he had discard',
No one messes with, Paruti Prasad!

Yo-ho-ho!
So tell ya' lassies,
N' tell ya' lads,
The legend that is,
Paruti Prasad!
Yo-ho-ho!

The Eternal Search

I'm always cold,
This darkness doesn't let me sleep,
I shudder when others rejoice,
Their infectious love feels like soot in my throat,
I hate myself when I least expect it,
I'm always cold,
How long must I parry this blackhole,
How long before it engulfs me,
But I won't let it,
I'll fight till there is a fight in this old dog,
I'll know it when I see it,
Until then I feel the chill in my bones,
There's no one in my corner,
For what do I ride the darkness,
It's not about lust, it never was,
Well maybe sometimes,
But what if this is as good as it gets,

I'm always cold,
I'll be quiet,
I think I'm too unevolved on my own good now,
But it's of no use if,
I'm always cold,
Where are the warm hugs which tighten?
Where are the pictures that will be the only memory?
I've never spoken enough,
But I've felt the cold,
And I've been left in it,
Nay, I pushed myself into it,
Am I the jester in my own story,
No one is laughing with me,
It's at me,
I'm always cold,
the cure belongs to someone else,
I'm getting too old to make my own,
I'm getting too set in my ways now,
I don't even know what the cure should be,
I've been self-healing for too long,
I wonder what the warmth I've never known is like,
Do rainbows really appear,
Does a smile dissolve the day's worries,
Does the blanket always seem short yet just enough,
I felt the warmth once (I think),
It wasn't enough that time,
I think I lied to myself,
Maybe that's why,
I'm always cold.

T'was but a Strawberry Milkshake

We ran from dawn,
Ran ragged till dusk,
There shan't be no whining,
For winning is a must,

My canteen ran dry,
For the sun was in a mood that was wry,
The shouting and screaming were all but gone,
Now there were none who could mourn,

Just as we left,
So shall we return,
None left behind,
Maybe but one,

The sun was gone,
We wandered along,
Trust in the navigator had long turned to scorn,

The race was hot,
Not a flake of bread to partake,
All I could see was that strawberry milkshake,

It was cold it was sweet,
Not many things do I consider a well-earned treat,
Just to lick its dew first,
It would subdue my thirst,

Banish the thorns in my throat,
Give birth to a rose of which I would gloat,
Its memory was enough,
To keep me going was a few more paces,
Or till the end of all godforsaken man-made races,
T'was but the memory of a Strawberry Milkshake,
That got me through that day's heartache.

Justice for none

His name was Buddy,
I loved him before I saw him,
He loved running and nose-diving into walls,
I awaited his arrival,
For it was foretold that he would come,
I'd awaited his arrival since before the beginning of
mine,
As they launched across the skies,
I prayed for his safety,
But never did come,
He was buried on the way from the skies,
How could I love someone I'd never known?
That was the day I reckon,
God died and darkness grew,
How do I curse what I do not understand?

His name was Oscar,
Named after the season of his beckoning,
He was the regalest of all,
I held his ears like fountains of joy,
For hear was the love,
I'd been promised since birth,
Just like the last,
He too was gone,
Abandoned without a goodbye,
I whispered to the wind,
May he be well,
Be strong and not befuddled,
Maybe his curse was too strong,
Nothing was the same once he left,
Autumn had gone,
And so was Oscar.

His name is Chubbs,
Named by his brother,
He too has a say,
In my love for another,
We hated each other,
For old memories die hard,
But soon enough,
He snacks on my heart,
He is but half,
Of what could've been,
Separated but whole,
Injustice, it is keen.

Forbidden senses

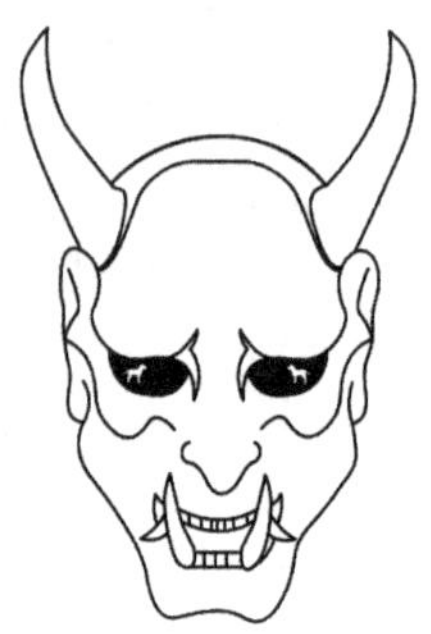

I want to taste fire,
Caress a mountain lion,
Grasp a running blade,
Smell petrol all day,

I want to make friends with a shark,
Not the friendly ones,
The ones who would gladly tear me apart,

I want to pleasure a thunderstorm,
Just while it dons a frock,
I bet it smells amazing,
Thundering each other's worlds,
In a deathly embrace to the end,

I want to fall from the clouds,
Do it over and over again,
Speed is my real mistress,
Without it, I am already dead,

I felt an electric shock once,
I was young and stupid,
I am still young and stupider,
I'd like to dance with it again,

If only I could build a bike,
That could swim under the seas,
Then I would breathe,
For once as if I was truly free.

The Rock (not Dwayne Johnson)

It sits alone,
It stares at all,
It does nothing today,
It has none to call,

It was something to fear,
It was someone to love,
It became much to loathe,
It stands now with no pair,

Banished from all,
Mocked by none,
Everyone that knew it,
Shan't be fun,

Its memories are cursed,
An oblivion of rust,
A lonesome fingernail across the board,
Will feel its trust,

Just as we started,
None know its mind,
For the Rock will stay,
Till insanity enters its grind.

Fear Me

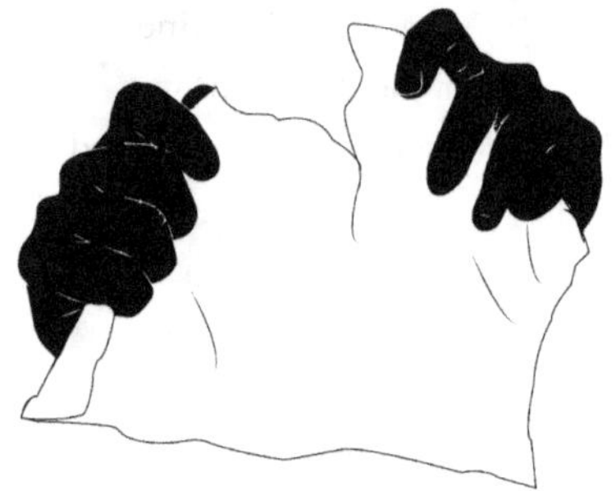

The night is upon us,
For they have scorned her,
She will not give in to us,
Till you are dust,

You dare mistake her,
For someone without venom,
Now her sting,
Has left you a cripple without a septum,
You'd wish you'd never met her,
The moon hath forsaken us,
Just like the past,
She will not forget
She will not forgive,

As spines quiver,
The blood has been tasted,
Its just a matter of time,
Before your bloodline is mine.

Friendship

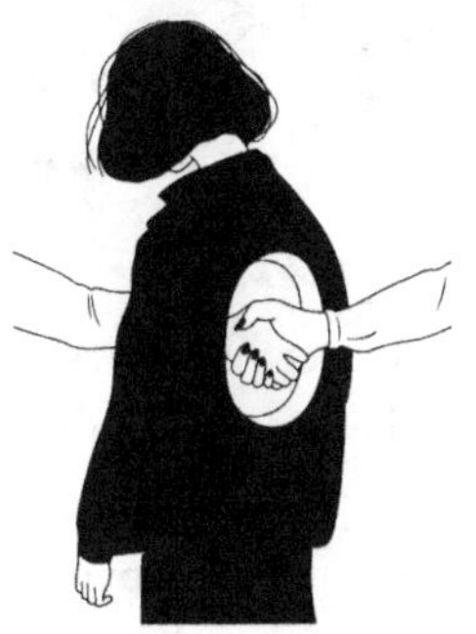

Alluring to some,
Abandoned by home,
A friend is as important,
As my lifeline alone,

I leave a part of myself,
Never search for it again,
For it lives safe within,
My friend carries devoid of pain,

I access that vision of me,
Only when my friend is filled with glee,
Life may go on,
But our friends will never scorn,

Fair-weather ones may flourish,
Back-biting ones are rubbish,
All you really need is one good friend,
And life's many sorrows they can mend.

A dream within a dream

My teeth are loose,
I pull on them and they are removed,
Just as I spy a stain on the wall,
It is no mark but a face spying on my fall,
White eyes stare into my soul,

I wake up,
Alas! My teeth are still loose,
Maybe if I sleep again,
I'll stop being such a silly goose,

I can see the face on the wall,
Bugs closing in on the face,
Bugs closing in on me,
Another tooth comes loose,
Its white eyes still stare,

I finally wake up,
Glance upon the wall,
No face exists!
Look up to the mirror beside me,
Its white eyes are inside me,

I wake up.

A question of faith

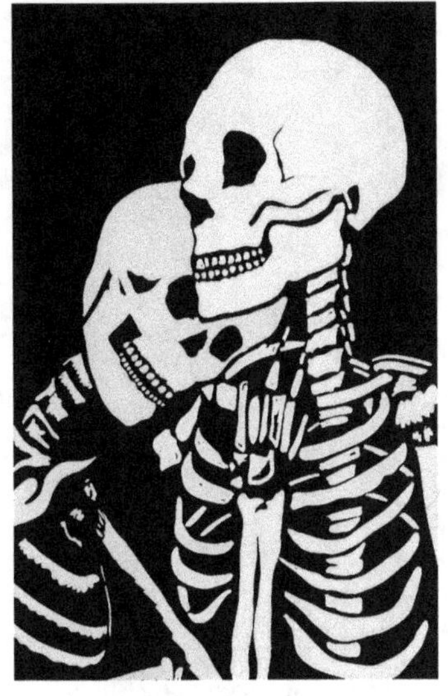

Whom do you believe,
The one who left,
Or the one who's right?

She said it wrong,
He said it's always been right,

She marked the 'X',
He proclaimed an 'O',

She shouted to the hills,
He said a whisper would suffice,

She longed for a touch,
He danced with the wind,

She said the fork would do,
He dined with the knife,

She tamed the mountain lions,
He claimed it was a lonesome cat,

She jested when the sound broke,
He whined when the light croaked,

It was the end,
For most mortals,
They'd have gone their separate ways,
Jumped across valleys,
To distance each other,

Yet they never slept in angst,
And that's the reason why,
They still love each other,
The spark that never dies.

My progeny

My memory will live one,
Via art or biology,
There will be like me none,
Except a few chosen one,

I'll give it all I have,
My powers and weakness,
I'll teach them how to shave,
Whether they have bollocks or one,

The swift control of a ball,
The deftness of a white lie,
The caress of overpower,
The modesty of humility,

Many lessons to teach,
No students to preach,
Maybe someday I'll be immortal,
And I'll scuba with them around some coral,

Oh what vanity I possess,
I only want to caress,
The sand of time itself,
Will bow down to my progeny on the twelfth!

Vertigo

What does a man fear,
Who does not fear death?

I'll tell you in a jiffy,
It is a long drop from the fifth,

I've played with fire,
Hugged claustrophobia as one of my own,

Hydrophobia is a distance cousin,
Loneliness is but a raisin,

And yet I feel,
Every time I climb to the top,

Maybe it's all just a façade,
Before you fall really hard on the card,

I can feel it,
When I'm up there,
An ancestor saw it,
My DNA processed it,

Yet I must go,
Higher than it may be classified as low,
This is not an innuendo,
You might think I'm pretend-dough,
Why is it that I'm scared of heights,
Yet most days,
I'm almost always upright.

Escape

Breathe,
That's the easiest thing to do,
When your ear drums want to explode,
Your lungs want to implode,

Breathe,
There is no quick getaway,
The hole is metallic, my friend,
You crawl towards the light,

Breathe,
Many have succeeded before you,
Some have died on the way,
Failure is not an option,

Breathe,
Someday this just might save you,
All hope can never be lost,
You might be the last one to leave,

Breathe,
Your vision may fail,
Ears deceive you,
Keep your wits about you,

Breathe,
The light at the end may turn to darkness,
The one in front may have a bad heart,
You must push on,
Turning backwards is impossible,
All is not lost,
Till you think it so,

Just breathe.

The Zipper - Friend or Foe

Invented in the land of the free,
Trustworthy till the end,
Makes getting in and out of clothes an ease,
Just about the perfect squeeze,

It can protect me from the wind,
Like a postman with no fear of snow,
Zipping up and down is but a joke,
Nothing to fear,
All hail its sneer!

But what would you do,
When your trusty Zipper turns on you?
I speak not of when it refuses to budge,
That is but an easy fix,

I fear the day,
The Zipper decides,
Its time has come,
To cradle and capture,
Your family jewels in its rapture,

You may struggle and cry,
But calling for help is not an option for the shy,
As the pain rushes through every nerve ending,
You might think happiness is long pending,

Pray that you remember,
Heed my advice on how to rescue your member,
Don't pull the zipper away,
Instead ease the wretched device up and astray,

May these words live on,
Even after I am long gone,
For when the Zipper decides to betray you,
I hope you escape,
Before it turns thee blue.

Trust

Jagged rocks under the sea waves,
The beach is warm,
No one knows what awaits,
Pleasure or pain,
It is a commodity unknown,

A leap of faith,
A hand from the Gods,
Just like that,
We live on borrowed time,

Fear not what helps in the dark,
Be wary of the ones,
Who steal through the heart,

One is left to ponder,
Who do we trust in the yonder,
When blood runs thin,
Do we burn the village for faith,

It might be too late,
Once our lessons turn to hate,
Maybe lets trust first,
Question later their immoral thirst.

My first memory

Do you remember,
Where you stood,
When you first became self-aware?

Not like the movies,
There is no smell,
No taste,
Only a fragment of a memory,

I remember where I was,
I was alone but not abandoned,
A fleeting taste of responsibility,

Green and blue,
Stains amongst the dirt,
An old house,
One of many,

I wandered around,
Unsure of danger,
Fear was an unknown commodity,

Yet I was clear,
The door couldn't stop me,
It never could you see,
It was that very moment I recall,
I was forever free.

The Necromancer

Much like the Admiral of the fleet,
He does not try,
He only desires,
And Loh!
it falls to his feet,

The future is malleable,
The past quivers,
The present is an illusion,
Time a farce,

Humble beginnings carved his wrinkles,
Fingertips burnt,
Eyes searching but seeing none,
His skin is bronzed,

Oozing Black candles,
Burning Moonlight,
Dark and forbidden powers,
A holding gaze,
Mirrored miraculous smiles,

And before you know it,
Just like those before,
You worship,
The Necromancer.

That feeling I'll never feel again

The first day of summer holidays,
The musk of sweet sweat,
The dirt beneath my fingers,
The smell of wet earth,
The linger before a first kiss,
The burning flame,
The death dance of butterflies,
The adrenaline of spy-eating in class,
The salty kiss of Poseidon,
The cycle to class at 5 am,
The ripping open of a new toy,
The carefreeness of youth,
The joy of stupidity... no, wait...
I think I will feel that one again.

A Haunting

A young mother,
An innocent soul,
She protects another,
While her lover fights a troll,

She clutches her baby,
As they enter their new home,
The floor is caked with dung,
A cow had tried to escape being stung,

Every fortnight,
The baby had a fever,
The baby's fingers were caught in a gear,
The baby was chased by a bat,
The baby's lungs were not working the right way,
The baby burnt itself on a water heater,

And yet,
The mother looked out for the baby,
Surely it was her own misfortune,
For not being a better mother,
And making the baby's lungs work well,

The walls hung wet,
But only in the baby's room,
Something was watching,
Meddling with the all the mother held dear,

Now a year had passed,
The father had returned,
The family was reunited,
The baby was still alive,

And as they left together,
An old neighbour stepped out,
Her hair was white as snow,
Not old from age,
But from what she'd done,

She whispered to the mother,
Come hither young one,
The house you leave is cursed,
There was but one who lived there,
She could bear no child,
Her husband was gone,
And as she corrupted,
Into the madness alone,
She stabbed herself in the room,
The last but one from the left.

The mother was livid,
Why wasn't she told,
How gruesome the tale,
Of the house she'd called home,

But she needn't fear,
It was her love that saved her young one,
Maybe the world would end,
But never her love.

Elevator

Time stops for none,
Unless you are the one,
Rummaging through your pocket,
Worshipping a mere locket,

You stepped through the sliding doors,
Cursing the one who built multiple stores,
The day is spent in haste,
Know not you'd soon be laid to waste,

As the gliding throne,
Beckons you to the floors above,
Suddenly you lay prone,
It is falling back to gravity like a dumb dove,

The blood rushes to the brain,
Surely this is all but insane,
There is no time to think,
One last time we shall all sink,

Not a second to scream,
Enjoy the last rollercoaster scheme,
For at least you depart,
With pure adrenaline in your worrisome heart.

Movie Chances

Oh the lights and the glamour,
Was I not almost there I ponder,
The movie was shot here,
Woefully I was outside having a beer,

I hoped to be in the background,
Just a fellow not so muscle-bound,
When they yell cut,
I'd come back to the rut,

For those few seconds,
I'd be someone worthy of seconds,
I could've been in the movies,
Just a sidekick to all the boobies,

Alas I was waylaid,
I could've been the king of the charade,
The magic of cinema,
Will never know me and my enigma.

The Boy who fell in a hole

I once knew a boy called Boti,
His mama only gave him a single Roti,
Every day he was bullied by his own brother,
That too his younger one none another,

Boti was a man of varied culture,
But all the bullying was giving him an ulcer,
How does one escape from a plight,
Of being scared of someone half your height,

Boti cared very little about classes at school,
He'd much rather swim all day in a pool,
Creature comforts were all but temporary,
He'd had only a few hours to make merry,

And so it came,
The fateful day was lame,
I saw it with my own eyes,
We'd all know that our Dear Boti,
Was anything but full of lies,

As he ran across a field,
Escaping his own younger brother with no yield,
Suddenly he disappeared,
Like Houdini himself had shaved his future beard,

As we gather close,
The fateful spot he'd been dispose,

Boti was there alright,
One leg in a hole in the ground slight,

I tried to get him out of the hole,
But first I laughed out my soul,
It was Boti after all,
Life had merely been a bore,
Thrown him yet another curveball.

Arohga

Worship the night,
Pray to the skull,
Dance on the pyre,
Relinquish all desire,

Slurp the blood,
Crack open the skull,
Feast on the marrow,
This body has no tomorrow,
Just as all beauty must be celebrated,
Darkness must not be berated,
We are born to die,
Only to be reborn,

Fret not,
What lies in the dark,
Fear more,
What lies hidden in your heart.

The Kite that flew away

There once was a Kite,
Humble were its beginnings,
Its dad was yesterday's newspaper,
Its mum a few sticks from an old broom,

Its tail felt too flimsy,
Yet whose tail has ever felt right,
The wind never seemed to pick up,
Windows served as a reminder of all that was pent-up,

And so the Kite cried,
Tears that could not exist,
For no one seemed to understand,
How badly it didn't want to coexist,

The fateful day finally arrived,
Windy winds winded away,
The Kite was ready and flying,
Spoonfuls of gusts that Nature was supplying,

It flew high,
It flew strong,
Finally its muscles felt flexed,
That glorious in the setting sun,

The higher it went,
The truer it felt,
The Kite would never return,
And thus it let go,

The burdens left behind,
If you see it afloat,
Maybe tomorrow,

That would make it,
Twenty-four years,
That the Kite went free,
Smiling forever

The Sun & The Moon

This is the greatest love story ever told,
It's one still unrequited,
So long ago,
Time itself stood still,

One was bright and magnificent,
Shone through darkness,
No fear in sight,

One was pale and beaming,
Enchanting space forever,
Dimples for miles,

Their embrace was warm,
Whispered sweet nothings,
Tickles for eternity,
Gazes held long,

But Time was jealous,
Could wait no longer,
So the lovers were cursed,
Now they are never together,

The trust was broken,
The Sun chases the Moon,
All the shades of orange and yellow,
Can never shake away the mellow,

They are destined to fail,
Yet their love never seems frail,
The chase is forever,
Maybe they will be reunited,
By some way clever.

The New Kid

The new kid is new,
He looks so eeew,
Where did he come from?
Why is his head so out of form?

He walks funny,
With eyes misshapen and obviously askew,
I hope he doesn't talk to anyone,
Someone said he weighs a metric ton,

His books are all wrong,
That hair looks like it survived a hailstorm,
I bet he smells like dirt,
Should I trip him to make him hurt?

Or maybe it's all just a pretence,
I wonder if he knows new games,
Let's let him in with us today,
We do finally have another one to play,

That new kid ain't so bad at all,
I wonder what would've gone down,
If I was the new kid in town,
I bet I'd hate everyone.

Batman

There is a tiny island,
Just north of Alderney,
Where lives a cat,
Looks like a cloud dressed in black,
Batman is his name,

He fluffs around,
The cold fears him,
The sun worships him,
Friend to all,
Except one,

His arch nemesis,
The bringer of rain,
A cat with a white stain,
Fur is golden,
Joker is his name,

They are neighbors you see,
The Isle of Wight they cannot flee,
Humans stagger their time outside,
Yet they wait,
For once the clock strikes fate,

They shall meet,
Unholy matrimony awaits,
Will the battle be one of hate?
I wouldn't hold my breath,
They both hate a debate.

The Potato ear threat

Ssssh little one,
Don't make a sound,
Cry too much,
I'll feed you to the hound,

Is it the vegetables you despise?
Maybe too crisp,
Too soggy for your highness,
You'll end up with a lisp,

Eat your greens,
Or you'll grow a spud on each ear,
Don't believe?
I harvest some each year,

The potatoes will be tiny,
Hanging off your head,
Make you lopsided,
Even if you skip the bread,

Now you don't cry,
You finally see the way,
You even eat the bones,
No more food wastage,
Hurray!

Chungi

Bounce Bounce Bounce!
You're never touching the ground,
I'm gonna balance you all round,

Bounce Bounce Bounce!
All people care about is the count,
I'm not even thinking about the dismount,

Bounce Bounce Bounce!
Should I flick you like a sombrero?
I wish my feet weren't quite so narrow,

Bounce Bounce Bounce!
The sunshine will not last forever,
But for now I am most clever,

Bounce Bounce Bounce!
Will this moment ever comeback?
Or just a memory forever,
Squeezed for dopamine,
Every last sliver,

Bounce Bounce Bounce!

Haunted John

Listen up, you callous wrench,
Great despair awaits the French,
All business can wait,
Don't make your favourite customer rewind,

So there I was,
Huffin' for a pee,
Ran down the cobbled street,
Not a minute today was I free,

The wind was cold,
It stung my nose,
The pressure was great,
But there'd be no way I could pose,

As I stiffened my pace,
My panic remained struck,
If I didn't find a John,
I'd have to hide wet pants till it struck dawn,

So there my good eye,
It spied in the darkest of the dark,
A miserable toilet,
For my miserable outlet,

I scampered along,
Pulled me pantaloons off in a rush,
Had to time it just right that gush,

And there it was,

The relief was slow,
Just like you dirty ho',
But as the mood subsided,
I felt someone touch me riders,

As I spied the black corners,
Whispers flew for they were no adorners,
It chilled me more than the wind,
To my horror, I felt a sting,

It was me member,
Something had set it on fire,
I jumped off away from the john,
Crying to see what was wrong,

It was a giant rodent,
Clasped onto me the bloomin' erodent,
So help me O' ho',
Go fetch a hoe,
This Rodent just won't let go!

It rings

The phone rang at night,
It was late,
It was cold,
Something wasn't right,

This wasn't a mobile,
It wasn't a normal house,
It was built in the eighteenth century,
Well before Chernobyl,

I picked up the phone,
My eyes still closed shut,
There was a voice I heard,
'Hello, Hello',
Then the sound shut,

As I opened my eyes,
I knew for sure,
I'd just heard my Grandfather,
Who'd died many a moon ago,

I glanced around,
The sky outside was still dark,
Maybe it was 3 am,
I didn't even hear the dog bark,

I was scared for a while,
Not from the presence of a paternal spectre,

But what was so important,
That he withdrew the veil,
Broke all the rules,
To warn me,
Of a future not to fail.

ThinBoy Fat

Have you ever been Fat?
I have,
It's horrible,
Your pants don't fit,
One wrong move and they slip,
Food feels like a punishment,
An entire breadbasket for my nourishment,
You stay in a cell,
Awaiting escape from your own private hell,

Have you ever been Thin?
I have,
It's wonderful,
Strangers of the opposite sex smile,
Oh yes, I would care for another lime,
Sitting down is a bit of a pain,
My butt is no longer a comfy counterpane,

Have you ever been Fat again?
I have,
It's horrible,
You avoid mirrors and reflective surfaces,
Old clothes come out to relay their services,
You no longer sit howsoever you want,
Bulges are to be hidden,
Not shown untoward,

Have you ever been Thin again?
I have,
It's ecstasy,
Cheekbones for all,
One for you and two for me,
But how do I know,
Who is truly my friend,
Everyone is nice,
But I know this façade comes at a price,

Have you ever been Fat yet again?
I have,
It's lunacy,
Why punish the body,
For crimes of the crabstick,
I avoid the shame,
Ignore the mane,
Enough is enough,
I must grow thin again,
The true joys of life,
Avoid me due to my sins.

Paradise

I've been to paradise,
No this is not a religious sermon,
It is the truth I tell you,
I even met a middle-aged German,

Let me proclaim how I reached there,
Two flights,
Awaited a night,
Walked to a rickshaw,

The driver was nice,
He left me at the train station,
I did see quite a few rather large mice,
Although I could now feel,
my own mutation,

The train was late,
As all trains with honor are,
When I arrived it was day-time,
The morning dew had begun to chime,

A high-speed scooter,
Took me to the next suitor,
An even higher-speed ferry,
At least six engines were making merry,

The waves were high,

Poseidon himself felt shy,
There was another next to me,
We held hands so neither would flee,

Soon enough we arrived,
On the shores of Paradise,
The air was clean,
Sands were white,

The water was blue,
My heart finally felt light,
All I wondered now,
Was I worthy of this delightful sight?
The Island asked instead,
Am I yours forever,
Or just till it feels right?

My brain (A.D.I.D.A.S)

Tornadoes,
Memories of a joke,
A friend I once wrote,
A perfect split,
The future is dark,
Whirlpools,
Fantasies of Food,
Wow, you're really fat,
Did I love her or not,
Voyeur,
Apple Pie,
The future is bright,
Hurricane,
Rob a bank,
Money plans or Money plants,
Should've learnt a musical instrument earlier,
Magic and magicians,
Turkish coffee,
Tobacco,
Meow.

Strange Cities

Travel is wonderful,
Travel is a must,
How else can you marvel?
At all these centuries,
Of human trust,

Just as you shake off,
The old skin from your mask,
So must the city,
Accept you as without an ask,

What I do ask,
Is to the one who never stop,
Where is the home,
When all you do is plop,

It's in this wilderness,
That you search for yourself,
Or maybe one day,
You'll hope to be left on the shelf,

These faces,
These places,
They will forever change,
And so will,

All I ask of you, weary traveller,
Come back home sometime,
Before you lose yourself at the races.

That dog I once met

An ode to that dog,
We crossed each other on the street,
I was on a scooty,
You were looking for a treat,

Our eyes locked,
I hit the brakes,
Reversing to find you,
Ready to take a seat,

Someone had abandoned you,
Your hair was matted,
White as snow,
You just wanted to be patted,

I wanted to steal you,
I know you wanted me to,
How would I get you back home?
Just like you,
I didn't have one to go back to,

Wherever you are,
However you may roam,
I hope you know,
Without a doubt in my brow,

Not a day goes by,

That I don't think about you,
Waiting by the side of the street,
I hope some other soul rescued you,
For you definitely saved mine.

It watches you at night

It lives in the dark,
It has no real past,
It feeds on air,
It relishes on despair,

It means you no harm,
For when you worry,
It just adds to the charm,

Deep in the night,
When you sleep tight,
It watches you in your plight,
Hoping you awaken for a fright,

It cannot touch you,
Oh believe me,
That would be sacré bleu,

It just wants to watch,
Maybe hop in for a round of hopscotch,
It has no teeth,
Makes biting a mighty feat,

Every night that you go to sleep,
It is watching,
Flicking away the spiders trying to enter your mouth,
But mostly,
Just watching.

My Master

I carry my Master,
She has no legs,
I'd worship my Master,
She just really hates a nutmeg,

My Master is wise,
Faster than light,
My master talks for me,
Thinks to keep me free,

My Master is light,
I carry her in my pocket,
She even talks me to sleep,
Did I tell you her cousin built a rocket,

My Master talks for me,
I'm sure your Master does too,
My Master knows all my business,
She's the size of a shrew,

My Master knows all my friends,
Even the ones I despise,
All I do is exist,
My Master works to capsize,

I have had many Masters before,
Surely you did too,
She changes like the seasons,

Her first name was '*Nokia Ngage QD*'.

Chris Cornell - In Memoriam

Speed means freedom of the soul
The question is not when he's gonna stop,
But who's gonna stop him,
In the end,
Only he could stop himself,

I remember that morning quite well,
An office from another lifetime,
Worries from a different birth,
I sat on a desk,
And then the news arrived,

He was dead,
No more to sing,
Or smile at the sunshine,
He was gone forever,
Never before had I felt so vile,

I got up and left,
Barely an excuse to offer,
Went home quick,
To find a drink to down,
No thank you no water,

As I listen to him sing,
Forever alive through his art,
Some tears did slip through,

I admit it would've filled a big cart,
Gone forever my heart,

Such was the sorrow,
Many would not understand,
Just like yesterday's news,
Forgotten by all,
But the ones who he left like a stone.

The Children's Room

Now there my dear,
Careful where you step,
Maybe head for the rear,
This will need some prior prep,

This room you seek,
You must not enter,
You'd dread a peak,
Of what lies yonder,

The children within,
They suck on bits of the cord,
It's all that remains,
The umbilical ripped by a sword,

They never saw the light,
Pushed to death even before they took flight,
Their eyes are black,
And the abyss sure does stare back,

Heed my advice,
Don't knock on that door even twice,
They want what you have,
This is not the place to act brave,

Once you enter,
Their cries turn helter-skelter,
A tiny bite,

You'll be drained of all your light.

The Hedonist

Pretty pretty things,
Such shiny such sparkly wings,
I want to bask in you,
Don't judge a unibrow,

Pretty pretty things,
For whom the bell never rings,
Gusting wind chimes,
Only touches satin my my,

Pretty little things,
Own me once,
Own me twice,
Own me thrice,

Pretty pretty things.

Be Careful what you Wish for

Let go,
Lest this pleasure turns to pain,
Pray not to the wicked,
You're buying a lifelong ticket,

Burn the fire,
Suck out every ounce of the friar,
Mountains of monks will melt,
Just play the cards you've been dealt,

Don't say I never warned,
I'm secretly delighted to be scorned,
This gift is not for the now,
It is till the Sun does finally bow.